THE PORTAGE POETRY SERIES

SERIES TITLES

Dear Lo
Brady Bove

Sadness of the Apex Predator
Dion O'Reilly

Do Not Feed the Animal
Hikari Miya

The Watching Sky
Judy Brackett Crowe

Let It Be Told in a Single Breath
Russell Thorburn

The Blue Divide
Linda Nemec Foster

Lake, River, Mountain
Mark B. Hamilton

Talking Diamonds
Linda Nemec Foster

Poetic People Power
Tara Bracco (ed.)

The Green Vault Heist
David Salner

There is a Corner of Someplace Else
Camden Michael Jones

Everything Waits
Jonathan Graham

We Are Reckless
Christy Prahl

Always a Body
Molly Fuller

Bowed As If Laden With Snow
Megan Wildhood

Silent Letter
Gail Hanlon

New Wilderness
Jenifer DeBellis

Fulgurite
Catherine Kyle

The Body Is Burden and Delight
Sharon White

Bone Country
Linda Nemec Foster

Not Just the Fire
R.B. Simon

Monarch
Heather Bourbeau

The Walk to Cefalù
Lynne Viti

The Found Object Imagines a Life: New and Selected Poems
Mary Catherine Harper

Naming the Ghost
Emily Hockaday

Mourning
Dokubo Melford Goodhead

Messengers of the Gods: New and Selected Poems
Kathryn Gahl

After the 8-Ball
Colleen Alles

Careful Cartography
Devon Bohm

Broken On the Wheel
Barbara Costas-Biggs

Sparks and Disperses
Cathleen Cohen

Holding My Selves Together: New and Selected Poems
Margaret Rozga

Lost and Found Departments
Heather Dubrow

Marginal Notes
Alfonso Brezmes

The Almost-Children
Cassondra Windwalker

Meditations of a Beast
Kristine Ong Muslim

"The capacious, tender poems of Wendy Wisner's *The New Life* range from the peach fuzz on a new baby's head and the leaky, weepy days of early motherhood to midlife, postpartum sex, and the legacy of intergenerational trauma. 'It's dangerous // to be a baby, a child / in this world,' Wisner reminds us—but these wise, well-crafted poems insist on the wonder and treasure of raising children, too."

—NANCY REDDY
author of *Pocket Universe*

"Wendy Wisner's *The New Life* is a stunning collection of poems touching on the collective memory and the complexities of women and mothers. Leading with deep compassion, Wisner sees the world through a mother's eyes, contending with impermanence and complex emotions. Her poems, exploring maternal love and loss—from a grandmother's stillbirth to the grief of 9/11 and Sandy Hook—remind us of the beauty of a woman's expansive empathy. Through the wisdom of Wisner's words, 'this is the new life // and I can trust it not to hurt me,' we find a poignant collection full of hope and renewal that all should read."

—KELLI RUSSELL AGODON
author of *Dialogues with Rising Tides*

"Wendy Wisner's newest book of poetry, *The New Life*, reminds us—frankly—that children can die: 'It's dangerous // to be a baby, a child / in this world,' the poem 'After Newtown' says. But the book also holds those stark realities up against the miracle of the everyday, like a newborn's soft scalp: 'Glory / to the goddamn / peach fuzz on his head.' Candid and sincere, sensual and grounded, this collection is an intimate and masterful examination of marriage and parenting."

—LISA AMPLEMAN
author of *Mom in Space*

The New Life

poems

Wendy Wisner

CORNERSTONE PRESS
UNIVERSITY OF WISCONSIN-STEVENS POINT

Cornerstone Press, Stevens Point, Wisconsin 54481
Copyright © 2024 Wendy Wisner
www.uwsp.edu/cornerstone

Printed in the United States of America by
Point Print and Design Studio, Stevens Point, Wisconsin

Library of Congress Control Number: 2024942448
ISBN: 978-1-960329-55-4

Cover art: "soil fertility - when springtime comes again" © Ryan Douglas
Used with permission of the artist (www.ryandouglasarts.com).

Cornerstone Press titles are produced in courses and internships offered by the
Department of English at the University of Wisconsin–Stevens Point.

DIRECTOR & PUBLISHER
Dr. Ross K. Tangedal

EXECUTIVE EDITORS
Jeff Snowbarger, Freesia McKee

EDITORIAL DIRECTOR
Ellie Atkinson

SENIOR EDITORS
Brett Hill, Grace Dahl

PRESS STAFF
Carolyn Czerwinski, Allison Lange, Sophie McPherson, Kylie Newton, Natalie
Reiter, Ava Willett, Cam Williams

For my children, and for Danny.

ALSO BY WENDY WISNER:

Morph and Bloom
Another Place of Rocking
Epicenter

CONTENTS

The New Life

Solstice

My mother was born
on the first day of summer, 1948.
Her mother labored alone.
Ivy flared against the window
shot through with lemon light.
That night, the moon was full
as it is tonight. In the waiting room,
her father sat in his gray clothes
holding his son, Raphael,
the angel. When the moon
dropped, the nurse let them in.
My mother's eyes were root black,
still adjusting to the light.
Raphael named her Black-Eyed Susan.
This was the beginning. Later,
the steady unraveling of a family—
the way a girl's hair unbraids in her sleep,
end of summer, her pillow damp.
Tonight I'm not interested
in that story. My hair is down.
Summer's just begun. I want
only this: to see my mother born.

Driving Home

The car empty of children,
rain pounding, thunder, hail—
I thought, I could easily die.
It was beautiful,
something from a dream.
Lush green trees heavy with rain,
branches tapping my car as I passed beneath.
I looked up and the sky was a drowsy, gray handkerchief.
The rain slowed as I got closer to home.
I parked the car. The baby cried
from inside the house,
and I walked up the stairs,
my jeans wet at the hems.

The Garden

Drought season. California.
My sister climbs the plum tree.

I'm on the deck reading,
long bronze legs stretched to the sun.

We watch our father finger the edges
of his blood-red poppies.

Bruised plums hit dry ground.

❧

Back on Long Island,
my grandmother plants dahlias.

Not in the garden, which brims
with pansies and wilted clovers,
wintergreen and laced with frost.

She plants my sister's namesake
in a cracked brown pot
on the picnic table
next to the old aqua blue telephone.

When the phone rings,
the whole table shakes.

Sometimes it's my father.

∽

New weeds spring ragged heads,
snake beneath the deck,
strangle the hydrangea.

Our father spends his days
knee-deep in mud,
pulling weeds, cursing rain.

He stomps through the garden
in his heavy black boots.

In our absence,
he guts the garden.

∽

My mother makes a cave
in her parents' den,
curls all day
on their burnt-brown couch.

She roots herself
in dank muddy earth.

No garden for my mother,
only dirt.

Miles away,
rain on my father's
deep olive skin.

꧁

My sister wants the garden wild
but our grandmother insists
on manicured beauty.

They buy flowers at the nursery
and carefully transplant them
into the small square of earth.

My sister is unlearning
the ways of our parents.

꧁

Our father squats in the muddy ditch
next to the rain-drenched mint tree,
trying to salvage
a handful of dry leaves,
enough for a cup of tea.

How meager his desire—
and yet, his empty hand,
his bear-paw, his rough skin.

His need rouses me
from sleep, touches my hair.

Every Night He Asks Me
to Tell Him the Story of Spring

I start with the buds:
magnolias, forsythia, dogwood.
I work down to the roots, how they gather
water from melted snow—and soon,
I tell him, there will be dandelions.
I'll watch you run through the yard
pulling them into your hands.
Then you'll come inside,
place them in a glass of water.
*And if there isn't a glass
small enough to hold them?* he asks.
We'll find one, I say, hoping
he falls asleep soon. *And if
we can't find one?* he insists,
stroking my lips with his finger.
We'll keep looking, I say.
And now his limbs
jerk quietly in my arms,
and he has unfurled himself from my body,
like all the men I've loved.

Marriage

Through the kitchen window,
I watch Danny come up the path.
He's handsome, skin tanned and flushed,
hair already lightened
on this first warm day of spring.

I have a husband. There is nothing wrong with him.
He loves me. He loves our children.
But I don't trust it. Not him. It.

Another Child

Laboring on the bed, face buried
in my husband's musty chest,
I'm certain the baby will be inside

forever, like a prisoner trapped in a cellar,
and I the keyhole from which he peers
with longing. I roar his head out

and stop, his shoulders stuck, then
wrestled free by the midwife's
cold, deft hands. Suddenly his body

draped over mine, the cord still pulsing
between my breasts. Out of the corner
of my eye, I see it, the placenta—

wet, shimmering—another child
slipping out of her hands.

Nechama

My grandmother knelt
at the foot of the bed
and pulled out a glinting
cellophane box.
Inside, a tiny pink dress
with a lace collar,
pressed, wholly intact,
like a museum artifact.
*This is the dress
of the girl who died*, she said.
Then, pieces of a story:
a ship from Kyiv, a sickness,
a dead sister, a new baby
born out of mourning.
*They named me Nechama
because I was her replacement,
my parents' consolation,
their solace.* Then she knelt
down again, and slid the box
back under the bed,
into its darkness.

Milk

We sit on the bed.
She lifts her shirt,
skin ashen and damp,
stomach concave.
She hasn't eaten in days.
But there's milk.
She squeezes it out
like I showed her
when her daughter was alive.
Fat, glistening drops.
Am I doing it right? she asks.
If milk is coming out,
you're doing it right.
It's what I said
when her daughter was here,
her warm, sleepy cheek
against her mother's breasts
while we hand-
expressed
milk
into her tiny mouth.
As I'm leaving,
she fingers the red threads
of an Elmo doll
lying on the coffee table
among baby pictures
and glasses of water.
I tell her I remember
that her daughter loved Elmo.
She asks if I would like a sandwich.
She says, *We have so much food.*

Breadcrumbs

My sister couldn't sleep—
at our father's house, away from our mother.
I tried to help. I was a child.
I told her the story of the children
lost in a forest without their parents—
the trail of breadcrumbs, the oven.
I was a child. I was tired.
But I couldn't sleep with the closet light on.
Inside the closet, the forest,
the children looking for their parents.
The sky outside our bedroom window
lit with breadcrumbs.
My sister lay awake.
In the dark she could see everything.

First Love

I'd forgotten how I would sit hugging my knees,
the bathroom sink leaking, the darkness

in the pipes, and how I would listen
to each drop fall, a bell

slowly tolling—shadows from that winter
jailing me in. I'd forgotten

the hunger, which felt like sickness,
which canceled hunger. I'd forgotten

my hips, the way I'd lie in bed cradling them
because for the first time, I could

feel them, jutting. I'd forgotten how
everyone seemed to know

how to eat, how to breathe.
I'd forgotten how he forgot me,

how I forgot myself. I wrote page after page
in the corner of my room, disintegrating

but writing, my bony wrist
puncturing the pages.

The Father

Remember that September when the city was burning?

I ran down Madison Avenue looking for you.
The phones didn't work.
I felt like a body

without a soul.

I thought you were dead.

Hours later, I sat on our stoop in Brooklyn,
a bottle of cold seltzer in my lap

and you—
covered in ash, came
floating
across the Queensboro bridge,
home to me.

Then it was spring
and you were inside me

planting the children.

I looked up
at the ceiling
so I could hover over us
and watch it happen.

Why did I fear
such joy?

Now we are bound
by the babes
who dropped out of my body
into your arms.

And still,
in my mind, the city

is burning,
our children have not yet been born,

and I am looking for you among the bodies,
the father
they will never have.

December Wind

Last night I dreamt I was bleeding,
two cold gushes down my thigh.

I woke up thinking, yes,
winter is coming—winter

and my son. But tonight
it's only wind hissing something

awful, and I see my grandmother
before she died, gray lips open,

the softest moan filling the room
then ending, and I can't believe

the wind is coming from the earth
I have taught you to love,

night after night gliding my hands
down your rocky body

the way Demeter would collapse
suddenly to her knees

and begin to feel
her daughter's dark descent.

I died, and lost flight

Yesterday felt like summer—

our son tramped through the field,
        a matchbox
                    car in each hand.

I am trying to locate the spaces
between dream and waking:
        his fingers
as he splays them
                    against bald blue sky.

It's June. I'm walking barefoot
        across the lawn.
Angie's wearing the sundress
            that makes her look pregnant.
I don't step on the bee. She doesn't lose

the baby: her mind
isn't twisted into spider webs.

(Stop. Listen
            to the rain
        puncturing the roof.)

I died, and lost flight—
            words from last night's

dream. I told no one.
I was a child.
Did you believe me?
I learned
            to hold the letters
in the roof of my mouth.

Then I brought our son to bed

while outside a moth
pressed her terrible wings
against our window.

By terrible I mean
                    precise—
how I slice through the living room,

a cup of boiling tea in my fist—

And you
obediently waiting for me.

Are the children asleep?
Do you believe in soulmates?

I died
        and lost

        California
where there is no rain,
only flight.

When I asked our son about death
he said, *you get shiny, then you get yellow,*
then you get broken—

and he pushed
                    his tiny yellow school bus
under the radiator
until winter was over.

Bainbridge Island

It's April. Morning and evening are cold
and cruel. But all afternoon
we sit by the water,

knotting daisies into wreaths, bracelets,
chokers. It's Dahlia's idea,
she who was named for a flower.

Growing up, I felt like the only adult.
Dahlia, the youngest,
was meant to be a child.

Our parents fought
the way children fight,
riding on their hungers.

Now Dahlia spots a starfish
under the murky water off the docks.
My son rushes toward her

and they sit together
on the rocks,
squinting in the sun.

Questions for My Sister

Did we sit on the stucco stairs
each night, hungry, waiting
for our mother, butterflies
pulsing on our knees?
Or did I leave you
alone those nights, digging
your big toe in red dirt?
Had I, by then, started to wander
through the bluesy night calling
a boy's name? Did I bring you
home a glistening handful
of evergreen? Was there a day,
just one, when we stopped desiring
together, staring with our one eye
into the creamy moon's skin?
Or was the ending more
gradual, pieces of me spinning
from you like dandelion seeds?
I swear, I always returned,
spindly arms raw from thorns.
I did not leave you for long.

Trust the Trees

Erin walks through the woods, cramping and bleeding,
the baby unpeeling inside her.

Levana asks, *Would you rather go home and rest?*
Erin says, *I'd rather feel this way in a forest*

than on my couch. I'm home on the couch, the baby
inside me almost done, his legs crooked branches.

Who chooses the ones who live,
the ones who die? This morning on my walk,

a cool breeze, dogwood fruit ripe and fallen,
splattered across the lawn, oak leaves already turning

yellow and brown. Eleven years ago, my husband
walked over the bridge while I sat on our stoop

in Brooklyn, smoke from the buildings,
from the bodies, already wafting across the water.

Erin's message to my baby is *Trust the trees.*
Interpret it however you want. I didn't trust

my husband would make it home
even as I saw his ashen body walking toward me.

Have Another

In the night, my son draping his heavy body
over mine, I think I should Google
what happens

when you don't talk about stillbirth.
I need to find out what they did
with the bodies of the babies

in 1943, when my grandmother
lay in the hospital
screaming—

Have another
was the doctor's only advice,
and whisked her home.

Seventy years later, almost
summer, the porch door
creaks open and my son

tramps out of the house
without a word. I scream
and run, searching

the tall grass and dandelions
for his body. My screams
hiss across the chain-link fence.

Dream of the End of the World

The children were separated from their parents,
and everyone wore numbers on their shirts,
like football jerseys. You and I

rode the train, looking for our kids.
We ducked behind a brown leather seat,
hiding from the *pop pop pop* of bullets

or cars backfiring—it was impossible to know.
The train swerved on its tracks,
our numbered shirts softly touching.

When the dream was over, I got out of bed,
peed, blew my nose, then tossed and turned
while both our living, breathing children

lay sleeping beside me. In the morning,
packing lunches, mixing water
into oatmeal, I felt solace knowing the earth

hadn't been engulfed in gas and flame
as I usually imagine the end of the world.
You kissed me on the mouth

and something like relief flooded
my body because the end of the world was over
for now. We could take our kids

to school and only worry about normal things:
if they'd listen in class, be kind, stand up for justice,
not get shot, tackle the shooter, become a hero.

After Newtown

Think of the baby
C-curved
around your body

in the dark
bedroom.

His breath.
His hair.
Don't think

of the other rooms—
clementines

rotting on the sill,
the slowly dying
marigolds.

Don't think
of the boy,

once a baby,
walking into a room
full of children.

See only this:
the baby's hands

crisscrossed
in front of his eyes,
bones hollow

as a bird's,
little fists jerking

on instinct.
Love him.
It's dangerous

to be a baby, a child
in this world.

Glory
to the goddamn
peach fuzz on his head.

House

I could list the losses:
my grandmother's sister
who died on the boat from Russia
to New York City;
or my grandmother's son
who died on the way out
of my grandmother's body;
or my grandmother
who died while my mother,
my sister, and I held her hand
in the room with a wall of mirrors.

I could tell you those losses
lived in her bones
which housed my mother
which housed me

which turned to fear,
to panic, to love as I pushed
each child out of my body.

But now the house is shaking,
the windows doing their death rattle.

Another rainstorm—
and I am inside
nursing the baby.

Postpartum

This is it—
sweaty breast, goopy eyes,
pacing the bedroom in the middle of the night,
baby biting your shirt, your hair, the red-
breasted robin screeching its first aria
while both children lie on the floor screaming—

This is what you wanted:
baby covered in hives, sheets covered in blood,
your blood boiling
and spilling over. This is night
after sexless night, his hands cupping your back
while the baby hangs off your breast.

This is both
children tossing and turning in your bed, your body
the earth quaking, city sliding off the peninsula
as you grip your children and run—

This is the earth in his hair,
the sticks and leaves he grabbed and bit, this is the dirt
under
his nails
     his nails
            his

This is everything
happens inside these six-hundred square feet
where you made
love, birthed two babies,
tore apart, tore apart.

This is a snapshot—
no this is real life, this
is what you'll remember—

But you won't remember the precise
angle of his wrist as he squeezed the toothpaste
that fresh beauty mark
those soft, prickled hairs.

The heat's on too high, the bedroom
smells of spit-up, milk-breath, dreams.

This is what we wanted—
holy children, love, loveless
my god, my hunger, my righteous—
let's sleep together always like this

This is what we wanted—
          oh yes, touch me like that
          please again let's make
          our bodies make
          miracles.

Lines

Blood in the sink when I spit.
Blood on the morning sheets.
Milk, too. Is that blood
on the baby's belly button?
Are those mosquito bites
on our older kid's arms,
or something worse, something
the baby could get?
Blood and milk, blood and milk.
How many lines can I write
between the baby's cries?

Night

The baby stirs
No, it's the wind
The big kid coughs
No, it's your heart

Hunger

The big kid comes home hungry,
lies on the floor crying & kicking,
hands & arms & face
caked in dirt.
I put the baby in the playpen,
carry the big kid to the bathroom.
The baby screams.
I cover the big kid's hands & wrists in soap.
I massage it in, scoop up the water,
watch it drip slowly down.
This is how to make this child
whole again, through touch, with water.
The baby screams.
I pick him up to nurse.
When the milk lets down,
I imagine my breasts
are grapes bursting,
or stars brought to light
when the sky turns dark.

Nightscape

I lie naked on the carpet,
the children asleep in the bedroom.
My husband wants to make love to me.
He's beautiful: golden hair, sloped back.
I'm tired. Thirty-five years of wanting,
having, losing. The sunflower
does its job, pressing against
the windowpane. Night is long
and arduous. Tonight, I'll have nightmares
about leaving my children home alone.
The roads will turn to water as I run to them.
In the dream, the baby doesn't cry for milk.
He sleeps on top of the six-year-old
who reassures me on the phone:
All is well. How I would like to believe—
I am a well of patience. I well
with tears. I am rescued
from the well. My well
runneth. Enter me.

A Week of Zen

I lie in the dark
trying to meditate

Every two minutes
the baby flails against me

Every five minutes
the bell chimes

Last night you and I
making love in the hallway
the children in our bed

I took all of you
into my body
swallowing the children

While he naps I dream
about sex   laundry   sock lint
on our older kid's sheets

Outside, it smells like ocean
acid rain   maple syrup   breastmilk
like the whole sky is saturated in

milk   semen   blood
his   mine   his   mine   his

～

Sometimes I felt like a vessel
sometimes a glass
slowly filling
with sand
with salt
from the ocean
        his body
something sharp
shattered
his teeth   his eyes   his lashes

～

The secret is
I wanted my mother
while I knelt there in the birthing pool

The first time
I gave birth, I was Zen

The second time,
I was Medusa
howling   splitting open

～

Day after day
my arms   my hips   my toes
stretching to reach the top shelf of diapers
then my body
hunched over the baby

Through the window
spring   snow

❧

When I try to lie still
next to his sleeping body
I'm chopping sweet potato
for tonight's dinner
eggplant   zucchini   tomato

There was a garden
I wanted to have
as a child
with my children

Now I am supposed to listen
to my breath
here on the bed
where I birthed a baby in September
I see myself naked
deflated   split
how perfectly   terribly
open I was

Permission

Some December afternoons, I'm given permission
to feel happy, my fingertips on your jeans
as we drive through the valley, flecks of snow
on the windshield, houses lighting up as we speed past,
my throat and chest like a fresh cup of tea
spooned with honey. All my life I've been chasing
this feeling—the temptation to fall into darkness
at every stop sign, every street corner.

Reading the News

If you tell me the story of the girl
shot twice in the back by her father,
I'll walk into this August night,

crickets chirping against my earlobes,
until they stop, just like that,
because I told them to.

I'll find the crows and pinch
their beaks between my fingers.
I'll make it so no one

can speak for her without
permission. The moon won't
follow us as she does in the other stories.

We won't get lost in the woods.
Instead we'll sleep,
the two of us, like sisters,

the silver breath of egrets
like knives against our throats.

In the Darkroom

Two basins filled with blue-black water.
In one, the photos come alive.

With a clothespin, our father
pulls them out, glistening,
hangs them on a string above his head.

My sister and I bleed into focus.
Look at us: on the bed, playing

with a hairbrush, sleep in our eyes,
hair striped in morning light.
Through his lens, we are entirely

ourselves, beautiful—*his*—
in black-and-white.

Listen

Listen to the facts:
It's a Wednesday afternoon in April.
The baby is pulling up on the coffee table.

He, too, will leave you.
Like your father did
when he left for California.
Like the big kid does every morning
on the way to school.
Like your husband does
each day when he drives off to work.

Or, listen to the wind
that rustles the magnolia petals off the trees
and covers the sidewalk in wild chunks of snow.

Midlife

When you stood at the top of the stairs
looking down at the yard, the bone-dry swamp
and the sycamores like fathers
standing above it all, did you understand
this was your life? Was that the sun
licking your shoulders? Did it feel like sex
or love? Did you know it was your heart
wildly beating and it would always
be this way: the black-eyed
Susans nodding their spider eyes,
the morning glories clamping
their terrible mouths shut as you opened
the door and went inside?

Midsummer, Marriage

This morning I watched a squirrel
climb the slim pole of our birdhouse,
hoist her shaking limbs around it
and devour—
birdseed sticking like glitter to her fur.
I have never hungered like that,
but look at me now, pressing my body
against the wall that separates
this room from yours.
I was up all night, the baby's mouth
stuck to my breast,
and I'm so tired I might die.
But I want you, now, dead or alive.
I want the idea of you
which supersedes your flesh.
Your flesh is burning, and the city is under
a heat advisory, which means stay
cool, keep the children alive and hydrated,
and make endless love, right?

Later,

while the baby's sleeping,
I notice the scratch
on his head, the dried blood.
Sometimes he can sleep
without me, sometimes
only while we touch.

I've learned to sleep
through his cries,
to latch him on in the dark.
When I was giving birth to him,
I thought I was going to die.
Now I lie beside him,
unafraid.

Hot Brooklyn Night

Standing on the corner, waiting for the light
to change, the moon sliced perfectly in half,
air musky with overripe fruit and a day's worth
of sweat, holding my sticky cell phone, your voice
breaking up, coming back, it hits me: I grew up,
found someone to love me. Now I'm on hold.
You're talking to your brother. The light
changes. I walk toward the park, and the moon
seems curvier, swollen. Your body always
comes back. Sometimes, half-drenched in dream,
I forget about you, then knock into an arm, a thigh.
On the soccer field, boys have kicked the dirt
into a thick mist. Someone will love them, each body
slithering into smoke. Someone will take that risk.

On the Nature Walk

There's only one boy who matters:
the one in the green sweater, pointy hood,
bright blue sneakers that keep falling off.
He sways as he walks,
bumbling behind the other children.

Defend him with your life.

He could wander into the weeds,
fall off the bridge
into the swampy lagoon.

Did you love him right away?
You held him in your lap,
staring at his steel-blue eyes.
3 a.m., and he would not sleep.
You thought you'd go crazy.
So you told him: *I hate you.*

Did you say it before
I love you?
This is a very important question.

Now the tour guide is telling the children
about a fallen tree—
how its slim roots
once sucked up water
and your boy
runs his fingers across
the gnarled,
black decay.

It's how he touches you
in the early morning,
his fingers across your neck.

Only you can know that—
not the other parents, not
the tour guide,
not the dead tree
lying patiently
in the earth,
so many children
rubbing their cool, fresh skin against it.

Skin

My son makes me examine the wound.
When will the new skin grow? he asks.

❧

Outside, a spring storm: windblown
red buds, magnolias, dogwoods—
my favorite flowering trees
shedding their petals too soon.

❧

Don't touch, he screams
as my fingers come near
where it's raw.

When I slide the soft rag
across the wound,
I try to convince him
the pain will go away.

Why can't I let him
have the pain, hold it
in the palm of his hand?

❧

As I jog, I squash out dogwood petals.
My ankles chafe against my sneakers.
It's raining again. I run

faster. My calves burn.
I should have worn better socks,
checked the forecast before I headed out.

᠗

When I was a child, people said
I needed to grow a thicker skin.
I pictured my body covered
in bandages, plastic wrap,
rose petals, peach skin,
orange peels, tape.

᠗

Where did the pain go?
he asks a few days later,
drifting off to sleep.

᠗

It can't be, I tell myself,
but already I'm seeing
something like fruit
on the trees outside our window,
the ones I can barely see—
little fists of purple blurred
on the highest branches.

Shedding

Today I stood under the kitchen
archway and stepped into
my new body. Pasta was on the stove,
a cold Tupperware of string beans
on the counter. But I knew.
I knew I would never be the same—
the way I'm certain the magnolia
down the block has lost
all its petals. I haven't checked
in days, but I'm convinced
tomorrow when I take my son
to the bus stop, I'll see them
splashed on the sidewalk.
What I'm trying to say is
sometimes your old skin
falls breathlessly off your body
in late April, as you slice
a cucumber into half moons
for your child,
and you just stand there
and let it.

The New Life

Because there is nothing
more beautiful than my son running
shirtless in the yard, pink chalk
streaking his chest,
wildflowers squeezed
in his sweaty palms—

And because he's impatient for more
cherry blossoms
to rain down on his head,
he walks over to the tree,
flings his arms around it,
and shakes—

And because that doesn't work,
he waves me over and says,
Make it rain—

And because, I explain to him,
the blossoms will only fall
when they're ready,
a wind catches, as if it knew—

And because it's now drizzling
ripe cherry blossoms
sideways, across my son's face,
his father comes out the side door—

And because his father
makes me feel blossomed
and possible, I believe for a moment

this is the new life
and I can trust it not to hurt me.

ACKNOWLEDGMENTS

I'm grateful to the journal editors who believed in these poems and gave them their first homes. Poems in the collection first appeared in the following journals, sometimes in different forms.

2River Review: "*I died, and lost flight*"

Bellevue Literary Review: "Driving Home"

damselfly press: "December Wind"

Glass: A Journal Of Poetry: "First Love"

The Maynard: "Trust the Trees"

Nashville Review: "Nightscape" (as "Marriage")

North Dakota Quarterly: "A Week of Zen"

Passages North: "After Newtown"

Prairie Schooner: "Milk" and "Solstice"

South Florida Poetry Journal: "Nechama" and "Shedding"

Stirring: "The Father"

Summerset Review: "House" and "Skin"

Sweet Lit: "Reading the News"

SWWIM: "Lines"

Tar River Poetry: "The New Life," "On the Nature Walk," and "Every Night He Asks Me to Tell Him the Story of Spring"

The Tishman Review: "Postpartum"

THRUSH: "Breadcrumbs"

This book took a decade to make, and a few of the poems were written nearly twenty years ago. The book was written along the edges of my life: through the sleepless nights and full days of the baby and toddler years, the turbulence of climbing out of a recession while raising a young family, a myriad of career changes, and finally—a global pandemic.

I'm grateful to the poets, writers, and editors who supported and sustained me over the years—too many to name here, but in particular: Suzanne Frischkorn, one of my oldest poet friends and the person who gave me permission to continue to be a poet even after a long absence; Erika Meitner, who generously supported me with candid career advice; and Maggie Smith, whose immeasurable wisdom and stellar guidance helped me shape these poems and this manuscript.

Enormous gratitude to the poets who blurbed the book: Kelli Russell Agodon, Lisa Ampleman, and Nancy Reddy. Thank you for offering your words and reading the poems with such care.

Thank you to Ryan Douglas, a beautiful artist, whose painting seemed to have been made for my book.

A huge thank you to Dr. Ross Tangedal, for selecting my book and for believing in it. Thanks to the wonderful and attentive staff at Cornerstone Press, especially Grace Dahl, Allison Lange, Ava Willett, and Sophie McPherson.

Big love to my children, who lived it all with me, and who bring me immense joy every day. And thanks to Danny, my rock, and the first reader of all my poems, always.

Wendy Wisner is the author of *Epicenter* (2004) and *Morph and Bloom* (2013). Her poems and essays have appeared in *Prairie Schooner, Spoon River Review, Passages North, Tar River Poetry, Nashville Review, The Washington Post, Full Grown People, The Manifest-Station, Lilith Magazine*, and elsewhere. She lives in New York.

www.ingramcontent.com/pod-product-compliance
Lightning Source LLC
Chambersburg PA
CBHW031250120626
46545CB00007B/2735